PENNY DREADFUL

Penny Dreadful

Shannon Stewart

SIGNAL EDITIONS IS AN IMPRINT OF VÉHICULE PRESS

Published with the generous assistance of The Canada Council for the Arts and the Book Publishing Industry Development Program of the Department of Canadian Heritage.

SIGNAL EDITIONS EDITOR: CARMINE STARNINO

Cover design: David Drummond
Photo of author: Michael Diner
Set in Minion by Simon Garamond
Printed by Marquis Book Printing Inc.

Copyright © Shannon Stewart 2008
All rights reserved.

LIBRARY AND ARCHIVES CANADA CATALOGUING
IN PUBLICATION DATA

Stewart, Shannon, 1966-
Penny Dreadful / Shannon Stewart.
Poems.
ISBN 978-1-55065-245-1
I. Title.
PS8587.T4894P46 2008   C811'.54   C2008-904257-3

Published by Véhicule Press, Montréal, Québec, Canada
www.vehiculepress.com

Distribution in Canada by LitDistCo
orders@litdistco.ca
Distributed in the U.S. by Independent Publishers Group
www.ipgbook.com

Printed in Canada

All the poets, they studied rules of verse. And those ladies, they rolled their eyes.

–Lou Reed

Acknowledgements

I gratefully acknowledge the British Columbia Arts Council for their financial assistance during the writing of this book.

Much appreciation to the editors of the magazines where some of these poems first appeared: *Event*; *Maisonneuve*; *Malahat Review*; *PRISM international*; *Room of One's Own*; *THIS Magazine*; *Vancouver Review*. Thanks to the editors of the *Weekly World News* that once graced the aisles of our supermarkets. Two selections of tabloid poems were shortlisted for the 2004 and 2005 CBC Literary Awards.

I am indebted to my family, friends and community for their conversations, insights and interest. Special thanks to Michael Diner, and Janet and Ian Stewart, and to my editor, Carmine Starnino.

Contents

Penny Dreadful 11
Fleet Street 12
West Coast Reduction Ltd. 13
Pickton Pig Farm 14
Piggy Palace Society of Good Times 15
63 Missing from the Low Track 16
A Rose By Any Other Name 17
Tidal Flats Housing Co-operative 20
Some of Us 21
Tête-à-tête 22
Debutante 23
Bête Noire 24
Keeping Informed 25
Witness 27
Gone 29
Reveille 31
My Best Tenant is a Demon from Hades, Says Landlord 32
Flush of Fear—Is Your Toilet the Gateway to Hell? 33
Roofers Find Bucket Full of Teeth 35
Man Jailed After Sucking the Toes of Three Unsuspecting Women 36
Human Owl is Driving His Neighbours Crazy 37
Gay Disaster Dooms Dinosaurs 38
Horoscope: Your Weekly Star Guide 39
Woman Gives Birth to Frog 44
Garage Sale Tycoon Richest Man in the World 45
Jesus Photographed on Mars! 49
Supermarket Lobsters Escape Tank & Terrorize Shoppers 50

Aliens Coming Back Home—To Earth! 51
For Sale: House Haunted by Elvis 54
Page 5—Girl Next Door! 55
Jane 57
Evidence of Missing Women Found 64
Inquest 66
Sawney Beane 67
Memorial 69

Notes 73

PENNY DREADFUL

Coiled in his boots
is a quick escape.
Black domino, hooded
cape, he leaps over walls
to visit a lone young lady
he claws to taste.
He'd like to have her
hard with sauce, in haste.
But her cries bring help.
He flies to a rooftop, leans
in oilskin, tall and dapper.

Spring Heeled Jack
The Terror of London
Splendidly Illustrated
In Handsome Wrapper.

FLEET STREET

A blood-soaked rag wraps around a pole.
Easy shaving for a penny—As good as you will find any.
Todd wears an apron. At the windowsill,
wigs of human hair, a jar of teeth with twisted roots.
Your tongue finds a molar. Strange to think
it planted in your jaw like a sprouted pit.
Recline, Sir. You just want a bit of polishing off.
Chair large as a throne, razors' moons of metal
on the wall. A growl from a corner of the room.
Todd's dog-bear sniffs your coat. You sit, hear a stir
of metal beneath your feet. The chair tilts
through the floor. Your world is upside down,
Todd's hair a polish brush of black. You hit
the ground, the ceiling shuts and all the lights snuff out.

WEST COAST REDUCTION LTD.
105 NORTH COMMERCIAL DRIVE

Pig-meat ; prostitute.
At the rendering plant
he dropped off loads
of entrails, bones, blood.
Machines boiled it down
to perfume, lipstick,
shampoo.

Who could read past
headlines so obscene?

We stood in the shower
instead; keeping clean.

PICKTON PIG FARM
953 DOMINION AVENUE

He had dirty hands, sat
for hours, saying nothing.
Patrolled his yard with
a boar trained to attack.
Trailers filled with purses,
i.d.'s, girlie bric-a-brac.
Drove a bus with tinted
windows, asked the girls
how they wanted to be
paid. Repeatedly stabbed
a prostitute but charges
were, inexplicably,
stayed. Some knew what he
was up to, but didn't speak.
Those women were poor,
life isn't fair. He was
a decent neighbour,
a quiet man,
impossible,
a millionaire.

PIGGY PALACE SOCIETY OF GOOD TIMES
2552 BURNS ROAD

Everyone likes a party, yeee-
haw, the great pig on a spit.
The bikers, the booze, the
music and dancing, not to
mention the missing women.
Of course, they weren't missing
until later. At the party they
were entertaining, taking off
their clothes, asking men what
they liked to do best. Lots
of things go missing every day:
keys, watches, teeth, sunglasses.
They'll turn up eventually,
you'll see.

63 MISSING FROM THE LOW TRACK

I come home, after groceries and soccer practice
to uninvited guests. A woman splashes water
in the bathroom, clatters jars on the countertop.
I tap at the door but she doesn't answer.
In the kitchen two women are cooking dinner.
I tell them this is entirely unnecessary.
Thirty spice bottles are lined up beside the stove.
The sink fills with the peels of vegetables.
A woman brings in the mail and feeds the dog.
In the laundry room machines churn and hum.
I can help fold, I tell a tall woman in the stairwell.
She continues up to my room, dumps the basket
out on my bed. Bright lingerie spills over onto
the carpet. *That's not mine*, I say. I have never
owned anything lacy and red.
The kids run screaming down the hallway.
Someone is counting slowly to one hundred,
her head buried in her arms. In my office
a woman pulls books from the shelves
and reads them voraciously. She devours a novel
while I stand there, her fingers flying at the edge
of the pages. *Do you have any romance?* she asks.
This is all so sad. Someone answers the ringing
telephone. A vacuum whines downstairs. I call
a taxi, and ask dispatch how many cabs are needed
for 63 women. He wants to know if this is some kind
of riddle. *Where you going to?* he asks. *Sounds like fun*,
he says. *Sounds like a real picnic.* I tell the women
to stop what they are doing. I take things
out of their hands; spatulas, cloths, towels.
They are reluctant, grumble under their breath,
jockey for a decent place at the hallway mirror.
They find their purses, apply lipstick.
The children watch between the slats
of the banister, waving goodbye.
The women leave in a cloud of mint and powder,
the drivers behind their wheels, smiling.

A ROSE BY ANY OTHER NAME

i. Cow

Under a Holstein coat
teats drip
perpetual maternity.
In other lands
I am worshipped,
painted, wrapped in silk.
Not stupid at all,
but Bovine—
Mother of Milk.

ii. Slut

Because I fuck
and fuck well.
Because one
is never enough.
Because I prefer not
to wear undergarments
or keep the prim
protocols of
ladyhood. Yeah,
I'm a slut. No
if, and or—
Nice butt!

III. Cunt

This grunt
of a word
you cast
at the end
of your line.
Look what
comes up
from the sea;
purple, wet
and manifold.
It made you.
Get down
on your knees
and kiss it
better.

IV. Bitch

If she's strong,
smart, thin,
vocal, rich—
she turns canine,
all paws and itch.
Not so long ago,
burned as witch.

v. Whore

You tell me
what isn't for sale.
I'm one letter
away from whole.
Take that R and rent
yourself a rope.
See what's happy
when life's
lost hope.

TIDAL FLATS HOUSING CO-OPERATIVE
1110 ODLUM DRIVE

At the co-op we had monthly
meetings to discuss carpets
and roofs, and how many
cats were allowed as pets.
We grew small and beautiful
gardens, cooked dinners, gave
birth, fought, waited for clothes
to dry. In front of our home,
women walked up and down
the streets, into the alleys, along
the railway tracks, in all kinds of
weather. They never complained,
standing in the rain like tall soldiers.
We visited the ice cream store,
stepped over condoms
and needles, waited in line
to taste new flavours.
We jogged, took buses to work,
walked our kids to school. No one
was worse off for the women
who clacked along the sidewalk
before us, who climbed into trucks,
closed doors and were gone.
We watched from our windows,
made cups of tea, carried on.

SOME OF US

Some of us whittled ourselves down to bone
and sinew and fished like that, hello, hello
over waters filled with weeds and silver men.
Some hung like tomatoes in a hot garden, all scent
and staked flesh. Some of us asked for food,
for cigarettes, for stock tips and just kept asking,
here or there, this or that, yours or mine?
Some had urges to bare breasts, thighs,
hard-packed asses like scoops of ice cream.
Some couldn't shut up and some were quiet
as clocks, the tongue's mainspring tightening with hours.
Some wanted it fast, wanted it slow, wanted it
hanging from ropes, darkly, explosively like
a bear in the garbage at 2 am. Some had pimps,
some had personal trainers and some had pavement
their feet flopped on like stunned animals and some
with this much pain in their face, their erupted skin,
their voice a country with lacy borders of piss.
And some so beautiful it took all day to appear
like that, radiant as jell-o, coiffed as a prairie.
Some of us were happy, some angry, some
didn't care, the stockings and little buckles
of silver at the ankle, pink talc, epilation,
gynaecological terrors, botox, divorcées.
Layers of us marching through eternity,
harlot, courtesan, geisha, such pretty
names, credit cards, syringes. Some of us
born today, knowing how to make wee fists
and the new lungs expanding as the foetal doors
of the heart begin to close, so soon, so young,
wailing for love.

TÊTE-À-TÊTE

The hog
invited me to dinner.

I didn't mind the bristles
on his chinny-chin-chin.

And the truffles by candlelight
were a definite hit. I hadn't

known the porcine heart
was so similar to my own.

Is it true, I asked, that you eat your own kind?
(I had witnessed it with my own eyes,

but wanted to hear him answer.) His wet
snout trembled over the china rims, pink

and blind. You must think I am a monster!
And dabbed a tear with scented linen.

When he did not come back to bed that night
I knew something was wrong.

Tiptoeing down the cold halls I found
an empty room where his body hung

from a hook, like a gorged tick. How
he had climbed up there, and cut his own throat

I do not know. But the blood fell at my feet
like roses.

DEBUTANTE

Are you hungry? asked the fly, proboscis lowered
over a carcass, sucking back his own elixir.

I placed my hand in his hairy foot.
There, there, he said, tasting me like that.

My knees shook as I straddled his abdomen.
We flew through the house, knocking

at windows, skimming the fruit bowl.
My own child opened the sliding glass door.

Swill, blood, shit's sweet decay—
The world! he cried, as we buzzed away.

BÊTE NOIRE

The tail grew first, a nude whip
I kept coiled under my skirt.

It sometimes came loose to drag
in dirt. I took it in my lap.

My lover stroked my whiskers,
my pelt of luscious fur.

I eye-boggled and bruxed,
I leapt about. It kept him rapt,

but strangely, he could not see me
for what I was. A pound of rodent,

eyes inky blots. He roamed the basement,
baiting traps with cheese.

There was a hole under the front stair
within whose narrow depths I perceived

cold winds, cobwebs, muffled terror.
It was not so easy to say goodbye.

I sang and sang without reply.

KEEPING INFORMED

Open the great
advent door
of the world
and out fall
the day's catastrophes.
Soldiers first,
easy to stack,
like rows of beans
with boots of black.
High on a shelf
in cookie tins,
we won't have to see
those warlike grins.
The executed
(so many today!)
float through jungles
once called home.
A shoebox keeps
their drift at bay.
The murdered
need lock and key
to keep them down;
the diseased sealed
in a Ziploc gown.
Don't forget
the exterminated,
the starved and tortured.
Open the cupboards,
clear some room.
Disasters prove
no end of trouble,
oozing lava, shards
and rubble. But special
thanks to the dear obits
who have their boxes

and fresh dug pits.
Our house is full,
all hinges shut.
We live! We live!
On deadly glut.

WITNESS

i. Gaze

For as long as you like.
Not much changes.
These are the twin flat lands
of death and desire.
You undress in both.
In both you expire.

ii. Look

They're not all pretty
says the girl, confusing
hate with love and it won't
be for the first time. The rows
of faces make her think
of game cards, plastic counters.
But she can't imagine
what sort of prize
could come from this.
How many needed
to win.

iii. Glance

At the headlines.
Flash of boldface
as silky stockings
slide over thighs.
What to keep
in your heart,
when it's all
for the eyes?

iv. Stare

I find you
in the mirror
again, face
turning strange.
You are not
like me, a bruise,
grey skin, then—
Here I am, alive!
Funny games
we play, my
silly sister
kept at bay.

v. Watch

It takes patience.
And there's time
to make yourself
comfortable. Not
a bad place to be.
Where a man
meets a woman,
bone and blood
will out themselves—
then you shall see.

GONE

A husband calls the police.
His wife went for a run 4 hours ago
on the trails of the North Shore.
She hasn't come back. The officer
tells him to relax. Says she might show up
in another suburb. That rush of adrenalin
and those new shock absorbing shoes
don't know when to quit.

A lawyer comes home to crying kids
and no dinner. Apparently, his wife's
gone cross-border shopping. She's likely
in Seattle, grabbing clothes off racks.
If he drove down there, he might find
her on the streets, with her windswept hair,
racing from store to store.

Three golfers misplace their wives.
It seems the women are jealous
of their long day on the green
thwacking balls into the sky.
They're at an underground spa
angry wives tend to frequent
when marriage is more sacrifice than fun.
They're dipping their toes into pots
of heavy cream and peeling their faces
with chemicals—best not to know
the details. They will return
when they are more beautiful
than swans.

A venture capitalist from West Van
does not notice his missing spouse
until the maid leaves cryptic notes
on silver polish and toilet rings.

He learns she has hooked up
with a notorious real estate agent
and will likely resurface in a far away city,
under an exotic name.

A professor loses his wife in the library.
At least he thinks that's where he left her,
but he can't be certain. Maybe it was in the park,
or the café? Or maybe they had taken
separate cars? Anyway, she wasn't in bed at night,
and he misses her singularly flannel dissertations
on memory and Proust. If anyone happened
upon her, he would, naturally, provide
a substantial reward for any information
leading to her capture. Or *homecoming*,
rather.

A boy scout says he saw his mother step
into a black van which began to roll
down the street. A violin student thought
she saw her mother hitchhiking on the highway
with missing teeth. The twins want to know
who's going to dress them for the ice at 6 am?
A statement is made that these are but comings
and goings in the wrinkly fabric of human migration.
Bipeds are quite capable of disappearing acts.

There's no need for alarm.

REVEILLE

The rooster tries to get me out of bed.
Cock-a-doodle-doos until I open
one eye, to look aghast at the rain.
He offers me his comb to brush my hair.
But I lie there, unable to move a muscle.
Other hens scratch in the dirt, gobble
for cracked corn. I paint my toes vermillion
and eat bonbons from a silver tray.
Perched on the bedpost the rooster crows in French,
German, Russian—Cocorico! Kikeriki! Kukareku!
I grab him by the wattles. You know
what language I speak. He sidles away,
a calico bouffant of feathers. So what?
I think and so what? again when a hen
fixes me with her ringed glare. Mornings
aren't my bag, nor are days, but bring
on the night with its tight leather sky.
I strut to the closet for hot pants,
rhinestones and a peck of perfume.
Let the others brood over calcium deposits.
I'm not that kind of bird. Just watch this
skinny leg strike the pavement. You'll
know who I am, cluck-cluck, from afar.

MY BEST TENANT IS A DEMON FROM HADES, SAYS LANDLORD

Funny what you can get away with
if you pay the rent on time, keep the
noise level down. D. Mon chuckles
as he throws his sack of garbage into
the chute at the end of the hall.
Listens for rebounds in the darkness,
shatter of glass six floors below.
He remembers the scorch of freefall
out of Heaven; the reek of flesh,
torn wings. Years of torment
and he's finally on his way up.
He loves this building, where
everyone's happy. Rules are simple:
post-dated cheques, no pets, drains
kept clear of hair and bones.
In the elevator, he drapes his tail
over one arm, rests a horn against a wall.
His sulphuric tang keeps most away,
but he manages the odd nod or wave.
After all, he was brewing Armageddon
in his bachelor pad—no need to be rude.
Only the frat boys down the hall
are onto him. He's squelched
a few parties as a favour to the landlord.
They are planning revenge,
but he's ready and waiting.
The tools of his trade gleam
on his walls like medals. What were
a few lost souls in the middle of the city?
As long as the shrieks of pain
don't go on past ten.

FLUSH OF FEAR—IS YOUR TOILET THE GATEWAY TO HELL?

You try to ignore
the signs. Yellow
crust seeping over
the floor, foul stink
buckets of bleach
will not quell.
You scrub and
scrub, anoint
the water with your
best perfume.
Plumbers come
to sniff the air,
refuse to help.
Then comes
the sickly mewl
of running water.
It never lets up.
You jiggle the handle
to no avail, Satan's
maw is open, no
stopper will shut it.
You grow too afraid
to evacuate, cross
your legs and pray.
You sit with a therapist,
trying to explain your
terror of bathrooms.
She asks delicate
questions about porcelain
and parenting. You say
I am not insane—
The devil lives in my toilet!
At night you stand
over the white bowl

waiting for the water's
suck and ripple.
You have locked
the doors, bolted
the windows. Only
the lavatory remains,
opening into darkness,
where the beast rises
out of the pipes.
With your bare
arms you'll push
him down the gullet
of your plumbing.
You're as ready
as you'll ever be.

ROOFERS FIND BUCKET FULL OF TEETH

She exists. Flitting about the beds
of boys and girls, exchanging coins
for incisors. But on this roof
something must have happened.
A sudden storm, a predatory cat,
or a fairy's old age, her misplaced
bucket of pearls.

One young roofer, all tattoo and brawn,
dips his hand into the enamel pond.
He digs and stirs, feels the bite
of baby teeth against his knuckles.
He remembers a lasso threaded
in his lower jaw, a door's slam.
Remembers fists, ugly snore of nights
no one could sleep, sobbing down the hall.

And how she came to his bed, all silver light,
reached into his dreams with a practiced hand.
He sprinkles teeth into the hot asphalt.
Stars in a black sky, they will guide her home.

MAN JAILED AFTER SUCKING THE TOES OF THREE UNSUSPECTING WOMEN

He loves how they bloom on the ends of
peduncular legs, pink flowers exuding
sweet ecstasy. They bunch together,
like bees in a swarm. Wriggle and
flare when dismissed from shoes,

plunder stalks of grass, hot beds
of sand. He loves their shapes;
hammered, square, tapered, lean.
The pale line of webbing in be-
tween. Loves their fat pads,

the lack of fingerly pretension. How
they clench in fear, get stepped on,
stub themselves and hop about.
They're his sweetmeats; his
Turkish Delight. Powdered

and coloured, ready to bite. At parties
he crouches on the floor, watches their
rise and fall over oceans of carpet
in open-toed rafts. Imagines
a storm, five varnished

swimmers overboard, flailing. It turns him
on. There's nothing to do but wait until
madness seizes him and he accosts
barefoot women in the park. For
now he dreams quintuplets,

plays This Little Piggy, with himself, in the dark.

HUMAN OWL IS DRIVING HIS NEIGHBOURS CRAZY

He climbs the hemlock
every night, who-whos
into the shadows. At first,
they think it a lark. Hope
for wisdom; mild prophecies
of gain and loss. But the swivel
and glare as they pass his yard
unnerve them. They keep
their animals in after dark.
All summer he squats,
wide-eyed and listening.
Teenagers shine lights
to see him blink, tufted sentry,
alert to bones of skull below.
He calls for names no one
wants to give.

GAY DISASTER DOOMS DINOSAURS

That's right. T. Rex was a fag,
limp wrists on that buff body,
the big swagger. He liked his meat
fresh and wasn't afraid of letting
you know it. Stegosaurus was a dyke.
Wore a plate of armour down her back,
loved to use her tail as a whip. Pride?
In your wildest dreams you couldn't
imagine a parade like that, the earth
shook as they passed, through the
steaming canopy of trees, under
the rainbow that shone with a crush
of colour. Same sex, your sex, my sex,
no sex – who cared? It was a Jurassic
jam of joy. It was awesome.
Only when the first rodent appeared,
gnawing and furtive, did things
turn sour. The great reptilian egg
of possibility was vulnerable. It was
robbed, broken into, sucked dry.
Don't talk to me about doom. I've
set enough traps in my closet
to keep those squeakers out.

HOROSCOPE: YOUR WEEKLY STAR GUIDE

Aries

*You should approach
your partner with those
innovative ideas you have
for improving your sex life.*

Under the bed
you've stashed
the warm jar of
chocolate sauce,
the can of whipped
cream. He lies
beside you, a hairy
slab of masculinity.
You are waiting
for the right moment
to begin confecting.
He watches
the hockey game
nude and completely
unsuspecting.

Taurus

*Try an evening of dinner and lawn darts
with that someone special.*

Last time you played lawn darts
you pierced your sister's knee.

Now you aim for hearts,
eat snails, make repartee.

Cancer

*A spirit-lifting vacation away from it all
is well deserved.*

You go to
Disneyland.
One daughter
shrieks every
time she catches
a glimpse of the
white-faced mouse,
the other throws up
blue puddles
of cotton-candy.
It rains, you lose
your wallet on Tom
Sawyer Island.
The last night
at the hotel,
after 8 Walt
Whiskeys, you
float face down
in the pool's
turquoise light.
Someone dressed
like Porky Pig
fishes you out.
Next morning,
at breakfast,
you look for him
everywhere.
A plump man
looks up when
you shout
That's All Folks!
But it isn't
him. You'd
give anything

to hear that
sweet stutter
paddling you
back to life.

VIRGO

Wear red.

In the mirror
you look like Riding Hood,
though not so little.

At the office the wolf
asks you to marry him.

Your grandmother is in hospital.
When you visit you eat
her untouched jell-o.

A nurse says, *Excuse me.*
Pulls the curtains
around the bed.

LIBRA

Romance is possible,
but you may find it
in an unlikely setting.

Which is why you are
smothered in the blue
clefts of a hydrangea
bush, engaged in
heavy petting.

Scorpio

*A weekend walk
turns into an adventure
when a bargain found
at a garage sale
makes your day.*

There it was, a giant
papier-maché unicorn
adrift in the usual junk
on a lawn. It glowed,
beyond glue and
white flour, more like
an opal caught
in the sun. For two
dollars you slipped
its hollow body
over your own,
galloped across
your neighbours'
emerald lawns, bore
down on small
tricycles, whinnied
at dogs. For one
afternoon you became
legend, a suburban
resurrection. Children
still leave sugar cubes
on your doorstep,
as proof you once
existed; equine
perfection.

PISCES

A trip to the mall
proves to be lucky
as you get an unexpected treat.

Your son will not sit
on the fat man's knee.
A buxom elf in red silk
hovers with a camera,
bells around her ankle
ring with every step. *Shouldn't*
the bells be on the reindeer?
your son asks. Santa smiles,
wants to know what he wants
for Christmas? Your son says,
Weapons of mass destruction.
Ho Ho Ho, says Santa.
Those might be hard
to fit down your chimney!
We don't have a chimney,
says your son. *You can*
just leave them
on our front lawn.
Santa winks, hands over
a candy cane. Your son
keeps it under his pillow,
dreams in a veneer
of peppermint,
the sticky sweet ends
to the world.

WOMAN GIVES BIRTH TO FROG

Okay, so she'd been a little promiscuous.
There was the delivery guy from the office,
the blind-date, Mr. Bow-tie waiting at the
bus stop. Not to mention the biker, and the
jogger she met in the park with the nice legs.
But a frog! She just couldn't figure it out.
The doctors wanted to know if she'd been
swimming in any ponds, or wading through
marshes? She imagines the nebulous cloud
of spawn glittering in the murk and shudders.
Beside her, in his plastic bassinet, junior twists
in a hospital gown, his rubbery trill the most
distinct cry on the ward. There is something
familiar about his face, those popped eyes
flecked with gold, the strong snout held high.
His throat pouch trembles when she rubs
a finger down the ridges of his back. She feels
a swell of maternal instinct, amphibious and
strange. Her son! Well, she'll call him Robert.
Catch flies for him, build a pond on the patio.
She lifts him to her breast where he latches on,
webbed hands clinging to her nipple. A crowd
of nurses watch in wonder as he sucks and
swallows, then leaps about the bed, focussed
and alert. *Isn't he something!* they say, trying
to take his temperature but they have to catch
him first. *You're going to have your hands full
with this one!* She does, a perfect mound of
green flesh wriggling between her palms.
She's got him, that's all that counts.

GARAGE SALE TYCOON RICHEST MAN IN THE WORLD

1. Early Birds

They're hard core, pockets
full of cash, classifieds in hand,
shuffling in the driveway at dawn.
First witnesses to the excess junk
of our days. We shun them.
NO EARLYBIRDS pitched
at the edge of our lawn.
Yet they arrive, sidle up in cars,
eating muffins. They prowl
backyards, press their faces
to the grime of basement windows.
They seek what we condemn.
From our garbage
they pluck their treasure.

Praise them.

2. Second Thought

She has not put a price on anything.
When asked about the vase,
the frames, the cushions she says,
They are not for sale.
Yet there they are, placed on tables
at the side of her house.
Her teenage son is ashamed,
leaves to hide in his room.
The woman carries things
back inside her home.
Are you selling that chair, or not?

a man asks for the third time.
The woman sighs, shakes her head,
disappears with the chair.
The people who have arrived at this sale
realize there is something very wrong.
First they are angry and then
they do not know where to look.
The woman is busy prying
salt and pepper shakers
out of the hands of another woman.
Let's get out of here, someone says to his wife.
And they do, as fast as they can,
having stumbled into this display
through no fault of their own.
These cups, these pots,
these ticking clocks,
upright in the sun.

3. Celebrity

Margaret Atwood's garage sale
had to be shut down.
Crowds clamoured
over her wooden spoons
and egg beaters. Two women
came to blows over a scarf.
The sale had not been her idea,
but her daughter's or her neighbour's.
They'd only wanted a bit of cash
over the summer,
had not anticipated mayhem
in the streets of Toronto, this clamour
for an author's throw-aways.
An old blouse is torn to shreds,
hands claw at a potholder.
Someone shouts, "*A paperback!*
With margin notes!"

And these are Canadians,
usually so
reserved.

4. Hard Sell

There's a little salesman in everyone
and this proves it, the father
out there on the street
riding his daughter's pink tricycle,
strands of costume jewelry
jangling from his neck.
He calls out to passing cars,
shakes the hands of strangers.
His children watch in horror
from behind a shrub.
His wife carefully sips lemonade,
collects the money.

5. Addict

When you begin to crash
toddlers' birthday parties,
circling the wading pool
in search of bargains,
take note: balloons
serve many purposes.
Don't jump out of the car
every time you see one.

6. Tacky

A toilet brush:
clear plastic handle
filled with rice.
Bride and groom
glued on top.
"*We took the plunge!*"

For a buck,
who wouldn't?

JESUS PHOTOGRAPHED ON MARS!

Folded in robes, like a delicate work of origami,
Jesus floats across the lunar crust of the Red Planet.
He looks down-trodden, tired of being flung about
the solar system, performing miracles when there's
no one there to watch. He's walked on clouds of acid,
tamed volcanos, circumscribed Saturn with a halo—
who noticed any of it? And now this trek across
the freezing desert, with only Phobos and Deimos
looking on, tiny moons adrift in the blue Martian sunset.
Truth be told, he misses Earth. He misses the dew,
the rain, the seas. He misses the people. Faces filled
with worship and longing. He'd forgive the crucifixion
in a heartbeat, if it weren't for his father, Mr. Thou
Shalt Suffer. Even him, Christ, his own bit of ghost,
lost among the planets. *Dear God*, he says, wiping
his brow with the back of his hand. The Spirit Rover
snaps another photo, astounding NASA. *What's he
doing up there? Saving Martians? Could Mars be
Heaven?* Speculations abound. And Jesus trods on,
through the ferrous dust, starved for love, for an ounce
of adoration. He strikes another hangdog pose for the
camera, he's always been good at looking disappointed.
There he is again! Is this a sign? A guy at his computer
looks up from a game and says, *We are forsaken!*
No one pays much attention, but the man feels a brief
thrill of comprehension, then gets back to business,
obliterating aliens with the stroke of a key.

SUPERMARKET LOBSTERS ESCAPE TANK & TERRORIZE SHOPPERS

What place is this? The sea
around them is dead, served
up on beds of ice. Fish eyes
goggle under fluorescents,
shelled shrimp a mountain
of pink.

Who dreams such iniquity?
Smoked, skewered, shucked,
filets of gutted flesh spread
for viewing. Alone, alive,
the lobsters plot revenge,
surreptitiously pluck
at the blue rubber bands
wrapped around their claws.

Grip and crush, grip and crush,
a plan of action forms in the
saline tank. Swimmerets pummel
shells in anticipation, long stalks
of antenna sniff beyond the glass
for the perfect moment.

They know the weak spots.
Digits, ankles, the toddler
left unattended in aisle 2.
Bibs and finger bowls filled
with lemon are shunned
for the greater muck
of terror. Only blood
will do.

ALIENS COMING BACK HOME—TO EARTH!

Rows of melonic craniums
descend from the spaceship.
We try to communicate
but those smooth pates
keep staring, black eyes
oppressive as an insect's hum.
We take them to our finest
museums and galleries. We
play music, sing arias, read
from our greatest works
of literature. Their hands flop
by their sides, slender chests
squeeze out a xylophone
of bone with every breath.
We walk them through the halls
of our best architecture, bring
them to the ballet, prepare
culinary delights. Green tongues
burrow into lobster shells
and roll peach pits about their
silent mouths. We wait for some
note of admiration, a telepathic
wink of interest. Nothing. We kiss
their hollow cheeks, tuck them
into beds beside our children.
Our pets curl up at their feet,
purr and ruff-ruff in dreams
of predation. The aliens
do not sleep. What can it
mean? If not displeasure,
then discontent. The next
day we try a different tack.
We take them on roller coasters,
dangle them off the face
of a mountain, wrap bungee

cords around their ankles, push
them off bridges. They tilt
their heads to one side, float
a bare inch off the ground.
We buy them french fries and DQs.
At night we roast marshmallows
and write our names with sparklers.
They huddle together, lobe to lobe,
eyes opalescent lakes. Again,
they do not sleep. We give them
warm milk, say a prayer, sing lullabies.
By the third day we are exhausted.
We rush about, short-tempered and rough.
We call each other idiots, drink too much.
We push our visitors from outer space
onto buses, hand them maps and some
spare change. *Go see for yourself,*
we say. *Have a good time.*
We don't hear from them for years,
how's that for gratitude? But one
night we catch a show on tv
and there they are—they've opened
a space camp for kids. A pod of children
zipped up in silver suits squabble
over the control panel of a UFO.
Our old friends look on, unblinking,
while a little girl tries to squirt them
with tubes of space food. They're
charging twenty grand a week,
for this chance of a lifetime, a voyage
through the stars. Parents camp out
on the pavement for days to sign
their kids up. We get a tour of one
guy's pup tent, nestled beside a mailbox.
He's number 321, hoping his boy
will get a turn before he's twelve.
The kid's in there, too, reciting
the names of stars from memory.
We turn off the tv and sit in the dark,

remembering those frail bodies
that came to us, pale sexless soldiers
out of the blue beyond. How hard
we tried to make them happy.
We floss our teeth, say goodnight.
Our dreams vast black holes
of missed opportunity.

FOR SALE: HOUSE HAUNTED BY ELVIS

Sure, you'd heard the gossip down the street,
saw a hound dog sniffing in the yard.
You figured they were only stories.
So what if the statue in the garden
looked a little like the King?

But what cause for a voice to emanate,
rise up the air vent by the chesterfield,
a dreamy slur from a bodega? It was true,
the ghost of Elvis lived in your cellar,
thrashed his pelvis in an orbit of sequins
down in the dank afterlife. *"Tell me dear,
Are you lonesome tonight?"* His croon
a shaky trellis climbed to reach
those heavy lips, pink as rose.

PAGE 5 – GIRL NEXT DOOR!

Clarification, please.
Next door to *what?*
Next door to the Implant
Factory, I might believe.
Next door to the Strip Joint,
the Playboy Club, the beige
offices of Liposuction Inc.
The girl next door to me
is squeezing her pimples
in a mirror. She sits
at the bus stop hunched over
her chemistry text, doodling
cartoon panels of Astrocat!
The First Feline in Outer Space.
She hides her breasts under
baggy sweaters, makes sandwiches
out of potato chips and cheese.
She picks at her scabs, says
her prayers before exams, kisses
mom and dad goodnight.
I have never seen her
wear a bikini, one arm flung
into the air, back arched,
a leg hooked over the rung
of a ladder. She does not
walk around her yard, pulling
down her jeans or yanking at her
spaghetti straps. She doesn't
smile very often, never wears
lipstick, her hair is dark
and shorn. The only person
remotely interested in sex
with the girl next door
is the equally bashful
boy next door, who owns

a pet rat called Orwell
and is learning how
to make a bomb
off the internet.

Let's just leave them
alone, shall we?
There's enough pain
ahead of them
as it is.

JANE

I.

Have you been a good girl?

KEEP OFF THE GRASS.
PLEASE DO NOT FEED THESE ANIMALS.

Jane ignores the signs.
In the forbidden garden
she creeps among the daffodils,
sniffs their yellow faces
for signs of trust.
At the zoo, she slips a morsel
of food between the bars.
A hairy shadow rises;
stalks the bait.
She's bad. She'll break
Christopher Robin's heart,
you can be sure of that.
Even the beast knows her;
paws each peanut carefully,
digests the pout and pinafore
with a snort of fear.
Jane rattles the bag in the rain.
Aren't you a hungry bear, she says,
reaches in her hand
for plush.

II.

She wears bright scarves, rouge,
opals in her ears. Under
her lacy blouse are nipples
pierced with metal. Locked
in her heart is a letter from Vanity,
the flotsam of his words
calling her *beautiful, lovely.*
Her bones bend to such flattery.
There was one who found her plain,
and loved her. She called him nice.
The phone rang about her house
for days, red blooms
in rooms of ice.

III.

Standing in the middle
of Hastings Street,
Jane shouts obscenities
into oncoming traffic,
slaps the fender of a car
that comes too close.
In a nearby bar, some Joe
sits nursing a beer,
wondering whatever happened
to all the women in his life.
From ponytails to high heels
he lines them up like beads
on an abacus, fingering the red ones
longest. *Another?* asks the bartender.
The man has a nagging feeling
there was someone he was supposed
to meet, somewhere this afternoon.
He nods and heads to the john.
Whoever it is can wait, he's almost
certain.

IV.

What I'd like to know
is which one's Mary and
which one's Jane?
The right is a little scuffed,
but sturdy. The left leans inwards,
half-broken, and the buckle's loose;
jingles over so slightly.
Together they are blunt, happy girls
romping under the desk.
Apart, they are virtue and shame.

I think I know which one is Jane.

V.

There's Dick over there,
waving and smiling, his face
bland as butter. He's getting
ready to run, though these days,
finds it difficult keeping up
to the flutter of pages before him.
Onomatopoeia, Jane taunts, leaping ahead.
Compound sentences. Etymology.
Dick begs her to slow down,
but she's off again, with a flounce
of skirt. *Fuck it, Jane. Fuck it.*
He lopes onwards, monosyllabic,
an alphaquad.

VI.

Inside the heart-shaped box
black papers stink
of something worse than
chocolate. The shining
apple leaps into her hand
of its own accord.
A pulse within
that spring tulip
vehemently pushes its way
into the light.
Like an animal drawn to blood
the red-room follows her,
punitive drama of childhood
she cannot shake.

She will never forget its draperies,
the shock of that large white bed.

Woman as an open locket;
arms wide, legs spread.

VII.

*It was in this reign that Joan of Arc lived & made such a row
among the English. They should not have burnt her—
But they did.*

Precocious at sixteen
Jane rewrites English history,
muckrakes the monarchy.
Sister Cassandra's medallion portraits
turn royals into innkeepers, fishwives.
*By a partial, prejudiced, & ignorant
Historian,* Jane begins, and promises
very few dates to remember.
Happily she ferrets here,

among base proclivities
and ordained marriages.
Every so often
a great lady appears
in a conflagration
of ink.

VIII.

Cannon fire over the Thames
announces the new queen.
Jane wears wooden clogs
strapped to her shoes
to float above the crowds.
Dutiful daughter, she does
what she must, takes
the crown for her head.
What matters her genius
now, encased in traitor's gold?

9 days.
The shortest reign in English history.

Please despatch me quickly,
she tells her executioner.

He lifts her face
from the straw, a bouquet
of blood and hair
wrapped in a blindfold.

Proclaims it enemy.

IX.

Don't think she's all biscuit
and bone china. Rogue banana peels
litter the tree house, a handsome ape
whistles happily down by the river.
The Lord of the Jungle is suspicious,
swings like a bell's clapper
through the trees, clang of deceit
in his cry. Tantor flaps his ears
back and forth, in misery, his eyes shut.
At night she kisses the brawn
of the Ape-King's neck, his torso.
Me Jane, she whispers
into the dark. *But
who are you?*

X.

Henry's third wife has finally done it,
a male heir tucked in her womb
like a cup of rich stuffing.
The Queen's appetite
enters its ninth month,
and Henry orders 30 dozen quail
from Calais. At table, Jane's knife
scores a miniature breast as her son
rolls in the soup of her hunger.
Her gastronomic smile
is a sentence. Life or Death?
Caesarian, infection, fever;
she will fall to such a fit of gluttony,
as to burst and die.

Henry's fat face shines to the future,
radiant as pudding.

XI.

Tag on a cold,
protruding toe,
make this final Jane
a Doe. Name unknown,
like her glance or walk,
now called for music,
or a vision in the forest,
that made no sound.
The breadth of her body
shines from a holy deep.
This, we know:
Her woods were dark,
and very steep.

EVIDENCE OF MISSING WOMEN FOUND

To this Jane, some advice: put more
of yourself into your work. Your husband's
three years on the Downtown Eastside
art directing a tv show could be helpful.
Try on his latex gloves, steel-toed boots.
Walk through the alleys. Observe details:
needles in puddles, knots of graffiti,
woof of a bus across a wet street.

That can of paint he brought home,
labeled *Homicide Green*, is something
worth looking at. Go to the garage,
pry off the lid and stir it up with a stick.
Green of trees in shadow, corridor green,
dumpster green, relentless backdrop for death
the camera gathers into its lens.

DNA testing. From the tag on a shirt,
chips of bone, a cigarette butt.
We don't need too much science here.
Enough to surprise, then leave it.
Know your subject. The farm, yes,
sprawl of outbuildings, the black gulp
of ground at your feet. The pig itself,
don't forget. I would go further, make it
this pig and not just any pig. Trying
a different POV can be useful. What
about the archaeology student sifting
dirt on the conveyor belt? Or the
woman in the new condominium
across the street?

I detect a certain hesitancy to get close
to the victims. Metaphors make good
companions in times of blood. A little
rouge, a string of pearls, and they can
stand up and walk for themselves, you'd
be surprised. Read those penny papers
for inspiration. Jot down the lady's name,
her solitary walk down Cut-Throat Lane.
Watch her hurry to her place of employment,
breath quick in the winter air. You'll
find her body beyond the printed page.

INQUEST

Tonight your husband
walks a beat
on Pain and Wastings
with the police.
Takes pictures
of rooms where
people eat and sleep.
Notes lighting, bare
mattresses, layers
of garbage covering
a floor. Running shoe
in salad bowl, tv
balanced on stove,
edge of child's arm
under winnie-the-pooh
towel. You think of him
standing in doorways,
the flash of his camera
making bright instants
of mugs, cans and boxes.
You think of your own
rooms, the time you take
to hide the clutter.
How, when you want
a photograph, you turn
to smile into his face,
your life arranged
for years to come,
exactly the way
you want it.

SAWNEY BEANE

In the dank black of the undersea
our caves reach back like twists
of braided hair. One is filled
with bones that scrape the roof.
Another holds the empty clothes
of men. There is one with
ladies' things I like to touch.
Rings of stone, brooches, combs.
And another where pots of brine
are filled with pickled limbs.
One finger rises, flashing accusation,
and sinks below to prod some other soul
who took the wrong path home.

The old sire squats in watches.
He likes to keep them wound though
the hearts that beat their days
have long since stopped. He plots
the hours of men on horseback
scheduled to return this way. We kill
so well by tic and toc we cannot eat it all,
cast surplus flesh into the sea.

Up and down the coast tides bring in
the carnage of my clan. A woman
plants her husband's arm in soil,
its salty cure a sign foul rumour is right.
We lie in wait along the quiet paths.
We stalk the shores in our bloody feet
and roll children's knuckles
over the ground for sport.
Forty strong and growing, our hunger
has no end. We are stains that stay,
even after the ground has drunk
the sauce of our men's castration
and the wind has filled its cheeks

with a bonfire of girls who could
barely speak. The woman knows
there is no justice. What she gives
this little grave is her own hand,
clutching at dirt.

MEMORIAL

We tramp through the muck. The women wind
police tape around my neck, a yellow scarf
they kiss with their painted mouths. A trailer
comes alive, its tin sides and cinderblocks,
a floor heaped with what is theirs; wallets, brushes,
bracelets. Someone finds a knife and carves a circle
in the air. She tells me to put my head through
and I see water alive with fish and sunlight
and a small girl rowing in the glitter. *Is that you?*
I ask, but she has already found the shore
while someone else slashes the air and another,
to disappear into a scent of smoke and clean rain,
pounding surf on rocks. They take my hands
this way this way their laughter a flock of chickens,
the snap of their fingers a wooden fence.
They have an egg and spoon race, zigzagging
across the field. One egg drops and a ladder
shoots from the ground. Up, up she climbs.
Another egg is a golden cave. One woman
kneels before a pig, opens his tusks to blue sky
and birds, a birthday cake with seven candles.
They dance now, swing their hips, sharp knees
rising, fling of feet. This is raw want, wild wails,
they hoist me to the barn like a bundle of straw.
Dance, they tell me. I have never liked to dance.
I try a solitary waltz and a child runs between
my legs. I pirouette, I point my toes, they are
singing Happy Birthday, clapping their hands.
They slowly run past me, in pigtails, in braids,
in sleeveless pink tops, waving good-bye.
The last woman waits, sitting on the slaughter board.
I have never been anywhere, she says. I give her
my open hands, and she takes them. I give her
my wrists with their throb of blood, and she
takes them, too. I give her my shoulders, my

throat, my ribs, her hair glosses to black. I give
my breasts, my stomach, my sex, and she grows
round and tall. I give her my jaw, my fingernails,
I want to be done with this. White teeth
grow in her gums, her shine of skin. She makes
me promise. I take her in my arms, this last
dance, and she rises, warrior, ancient and
beautiful, carries me as if I were nothing,
into the night, the cold stars. *Go,* she says,
and I do, the way we came, stepping carefully
through the mud.

Notes

Spring Heeled Jack was featured in many penny dreadfuls from 1840 to 1904. His bizarre appearance and ability to make superhuman leaps contributed to the mass hysteria surrounding his crimes.

The most famous character to emerge from the penny dreadfuls, Sweeney Todd first appeared in a story entitled *The String of Pearls: A Romance*. This penny dreadful was published in eighteen weekly parts, in Edward Lloyd's *The People's Periodical and Family Library*.

Sawney Beane is a fictional Scottish cannibal popularized in *The Newgate Calendar*, a nineteenth century crime catalogue of the Newgate Prison in London. Beane and his clan of 48 were executed for mass murder in the sixteenth century.

Carmine Starnino, Editor
Michael Harris, Founding Editor

SELECTED POEMS David Solway
THE MULBERRY MEN David Solway
A SLOW LIGHT Ross Leckie
NIGHT LETTERS Bill Furey
COMPLICITY Susan Glickman
A NUN'S DIARY Ann Diamond
CAVALIER IN A ROUNDHEAD SCHOOL Errol MacDonald
VEILED COUNTRIES/LIVES Marie-Claire Blais (Translated by Michael Harris)
BLIND PAINTING Robert Melançon (Translated by Philip Stratford)
SMALL HORSES & INTIMATE BEASTS Michel Garneau
  (Translated by Robert McGee)
IN TRANSIT Michael Harris
THE FABULOUS DISGUISE OF OURSELVES Jan Conn
ASHBOURN John Reibetanz
THE POWER TO MOVE Susan Glickman
MAGELLAN'S CLOUDS Robert Allen
MODERN MARRIAGE David Solway
K. IN LOVE Don Coles
THE INVISIBLE MOON Carla Hartsfield
ALONG THE ROAD FROM EDEN George Ellenbogen
DUNINO Stephen Scobie
KINETIC MUSTACHE Arthur Clark
RUE SAINTE FAMILLE Charlotte Hussey
HENRY MOORE'S SHEEP Susan Glickman
SOUTH OF THE TUDO BEM CAFÉ Jan Conn
THE INVENTION OF HONEY Ricardo Sternberg
EVENINGS AT LOOSE ENDS Gérald Godin (Translated by Judith Cowan)
THE PROVING GROUNDS Rhea Tregebov
LITTLE BIRD Don Coles
HOMETOWN Laura Lush
FORTRESS OF CHAIRS Elisabeth Harvor
NEW & SELECTED POEMS Michael Harris
BEDROCK David Solway
TERRORIST LETTERS Ann Diamond
THE SIGNAL ANTHOLOGY Edited by Michael Harris
MURMUR OF THE STARS: SELECTED SHORTER POEMS Peter Dale Scott
WHAT DANTE DID WITH LOSS Jan Conn
MORNING WATCH John Reibetanz
JOY IS NOT MY PROFESSION Muhammad al-Maghut
  (Translated by John Asfour and Alison Burch)
WRESTLING WITH ANGELS: SELECTED POEMS Doug Beardsley
HIDE & SEEK Susan Glickman
MAPPING THE CHAOS Rhea Tregebov

FIRE NEVER SLEEPS Carla Hartsfield
THE RHINO GATE POEMS George Ellenbogen
SHADOW CABINET Richard Sanger
MAP OF DREAMS Ricardo Sternberg
THE NEW WORLD Carmine Starnino
THE LONG COLD GREEN EVENINGS OF SPRING Elisabeth Harvor
FAULT LINE Laura Lush
WHITE STONE: THE ALICE POEMS Stephanie Bolster
KEEP IT ALL Yves Boisvert (Translated by Judith Cowan)
THE GREEN ALEMBIC Louise Fabiani
THE ISLAND IN WINTER Terence Young
A TINKERS' PICNIC Peter Richardson
SARACEN ISLAND: THE POEMS OF ANDREAS KARAVIS David Solway
BEAUTIES ON MAD RIVER: SELECTED AND NEW POEMS Jan Conn
WIND AND ROOT Brent MacLaine
HISTORIES Andrew Steinmetz
ARABY Eric Ormsby
WORDS THAT WALK IN THE NIGHT Pierre Morency
   (Translated by Lissa Cowan and René Brisebois)
A PICNIC ON ICE: SELECTED POEMS Matthew Sweeney
HELIX: NEW AND SELECTED POEMS John Steffler
HERESIES: THE COMPLETE POEMS OF ANNE WILKINSON, 1924-1961
   Edited by Dean Irvine
CALLING HOME Richard Sanger
FIELDER'S CHOICE Elise Partridge
MERRYBEGOT Mary Dalton
MOUNTAIN TEA Peter Van Toorn
AN ABC OF BELLY WORK Peter Richardson
RUNNING IN PROSPECT CEMETERY Susan Glickman
MIRABEL Pierre Nepveu (Translated by Judith Cowan)
POSTSCRIPT Geoffrey Cook
STANDING WAVE Robert Allen
THERE, THERE Patrick Warner
HOW WE ALL SWIFTLY: THE FIRST SIX BOOKS Don Coles
THE NEW CANON: AN ANTHOLOGY OF CANADIAN POETRY
   Edited by Carmine Starnino
OUT TO DRY IN CAPE BRETON Anita Lahey
RED LEDGER Mary Dalton
REACHING FOR CLEAR David Solway
OX Christopher Patton
THE MECHANICAL BIRD Asa Boxer
SYMPATHY FOR THE COURIERS Peter Richardson
MORNING GOTHIC: NEW AND SELECTED POEMS George Ellenbogen
36 CORNELIAN AVENUE Christopher Wiseman
THE EMPIRE'S MISSING LINKS Walid Bitar
PENNY DREADFUL Shannon Stewart
THE STREAM EXPOSED WITH ALL ITS STONES D.G. Jones